How to Survive the Cheating-mate Handbook

Elizabeth E. Lisciandri

ISBN: 978-0-578-16667-4

DISCLAIMER

The author of How to Survive the Cheating-mate Handbook does not claim to have a medical degree in psychiatry. All information in the book is based on the author's opinion and must be used at your own discretion.

"WHEN PEOPLE CHEAT IN ANY ARENA, THEY DIMINISH THEMSELVES- THEY THREATEN THEIR OWN SELF-ESTEEM AND THEIR RELATIONSHIPS WITH OTHERS BY UNDERMINING THE TRUST THEY HAVE IN THEIR ABILITY TO SUCCEED AND IN THEIR ABILITY TO BE TRUE."

— CHERYL HUGHES

If anger, confusion, self - doubt and sleepless nights have become your new best friends since you discovered you've been betrayed by your mate, then it's time to take a look into cheater-friendly phrases and attitudes that are impacting you right now.

Are you having difficulty trying to understand why you're in pain and yet you've done nothing wrong?

To add insult to injury, are you suddenly being held responsible for your mate's cheating or have you actually decided to take the blame because of worn-out, complicated attitudes that protect the cheater and make you the guilty party?

Attitudes and phrases that villainize the innocent party to protect the cheater are in everyday conversations that we take for granted, and yet they are extremely damaging to the innocent person that's been thrust into the chaotic world of the cheater through no fault of their own.

Exploring these carefully orchestrated attitudes and phrases that champion the cheater is the fastest way to acquire the tools you'll need to confront this challenge. If you inadvertently allow yourself to be influenced by these attitudes you will obstruct your best interests, and *this* friend is what we call self-sabotage.

Cheating can be analyzed ad nauseum; however, the final analysis, despite volumes of psychobabble, is: cheating is wrong and people get hurt - it's that simple.

"That which does not kill us will make us stronger"
Friedrich Nietzsche

NOTE- pages provide you with an opportunity to write down impressions that create a healing environment and also alert you to negative thoughts you'll need to purge in order to move forward in your journey.

Rejection

*"I **do** wonder if I wasn't good enough and that's why my mate cheated on me."*

Negative thoughts certainly will become self - fulfilled prophecies.

Feeling "not good enough to keep your mate loyal" is an industrial strength negative that kick-starts thoughts of rejection.

You might want to ask yourself what standard you have set for yourself if you feel you are not good enough for a liar and a sneak.

Think about that.

This is why rejection issues have to be tackled immediately; you need to get it right before this convoluted belief takes on momentum.

The truth is:

Cheaters don't reject one person for another person - they reject integrity.

Integrity - the quality of being honest and fair, the state of being complete or whole

Read the above statement until it sinks in.

The rejection of integrity comes before cheating ever occurs.

"Why does the cheater reject integrity?"

There are many complex theories on this subject and they're all loaded with confusion. Because cheaters come in all sizes, colors, nationalities, religions and also from regions all over the world - the environmental theory is unsound.

So what really makes the cheater tick?

ATTENTION

The need for the 'desirability-validation' is the impetus that leads the cheater right smack into a life of duality, thus chucking integrity to the wind.

"So, what part do I play in this?"

You need a solid plan, because the betrayal challenge is not a pleasant one. No argument there. But nonetheless it is a challenge, so the answer to your question depends on one of two choices that will dictate the outcome of this challenge for you.

A) Self-sabotage

B) Empowerment

"So how do I prevent self-sabotage?"

This challenge calls for a strategy.

The athlete mentally eliminates all impediments that will obstruct his/her maximum performance.

By using the athlete's strategy in this situation you will have to eliminate negative thoughts that cause anger, anxiety, loss of concentration, insomnia, stomach aches, headaches, jealousy, and revenge, all of which will severely cripple your confidence.

You have the right to be happy.

Get the picture?

Quickly replace all self-deprecating thoughts that pop into your head with positive mantras. Mantras are formable weapons used to negate self-destructive thoughts.

Keep in mind — it **is** your thoughts that will determine your outcome, one way or the other.

Example:

I will not give anyone the power to make me feel bad about myself.

I love challenges and what I learn from overcoming them.

I will be okay no matter what!

I am capable.

This is a step you must not skip because negative thoughts will take hold and become a self-defeating habit, and that's how self-sabotage works.

Entertaining rejection is Russian roulette; it will at some point kill your joy and happiness.

Notes

While caught in the eye of the storm it can be extremely difficult to keep a clear head because the cheater's game **is** confusion.

Be aware of the cheaters lingo that works against you at a time when you are vulnerable.

Time to explore!

"Well, if she/he were getting what they need at home they wouldn't cheat."

No doubt this phrase was coined by a cheater!

Nothing ambiguous here — this phrase states you're to blame for your mate's cheating — period.

Now apply this theory to a person that throws a hard ball at a big plate glass window, shatters the glass, and blames the window for being there.

"Yeah right! Why do I get the blame?"

Well when you consider that the cheater failed to keep their word both legally and spiritually, you're looking at cowardly and embarrassing stuff. Cheaters lack backbone and this is a prime example of it, they cheat and blame you!

However, a fact check reveals the cheater had the option to speak with you about issues affecting the relationship, **long** before they cheated. This check reveals the cheater's real motivation, and that was to cheat in the first place.

Accepting this phrase as gospel is aiding and abetting the cheater!

A cheater cheats because that's what cheaters do, and it has nothing to do with you!

Notes

"It's your imagination!"

It **is** amazing to see the cheater morph into a psychiatrist!

This is really old stuff and you'd think by now the cheater would've developed a little more creativity.

A feeble attempt to play a head-game with you is a pretty good indicator something *is* going on.

However it's never a good idea to confront a cheater without proof because this genius will use the "It's your imagination" comeback on you.

"So what can I do?"

Before you accept your mate's "expert analysis" on your mental status, stop and ask yourself what triggered your suspicions and go from there.

You've sensed a change - trust it.

Spending more time on the computer

Keeping a close watch on their cell phone

Excessive texting

Sudden interest in their appearance

Does not look you in the eye

Cheaters aren't all that slick — they get sloppy after a while.

Word to the wise is sufficient, get the proof before you confront or you may begin to think that you married Sigmund Freud!

Notes

"Cheating is a man thing."

There isn't a shortage of cheating housewife sites on the Internet, so this phrase has absolutely no basis in reality.

This phrase actually insults the integrity of the entire male population!

Cheating is not a gender thing, a race thing, or a religion thing, cheating is:

A BROKEN PERSON THING

Notes

"You have to learn to forgive!"

Now the cheater suddenly becomes interested in Christian values!

It's not wise to beat yourself up over the forgiveness issue in regard to the cheating-mate.

"Is forgiveness necessary for healing?"

Yes, but keep in mind that forgiveness has many avenues, and in this particular situation forgiving yourself for all your negative thoughts, your negative feelings, and of course your negative comments brought on by your mate's cheating - is also a constructive route .

Forcing yourself to forgive the cheating-mate may cause harmful frustration. So instead of trying to do something that will cause negativity, take the step that will produce success. Forgive yourself and move on, ASAP.

The quicker you put the negativity behind you, the better off you will be.

"That's going to be hard."

When you wake up and discover you hate yourself because you've allowed negativity to take over your life, that's not just hard, that's devastating.

It is your choice.

Notes

"It was just about the sex, that's all. It didn't mean anything."

This is another old-school method cheaters use once they're caught - minimize the damage.

Minimize phrases the cheater will use;

It only happened once.

It meant nothing.

It just happened!

Minimize— reduce something, especially something unwanted or unpleasant to the smallest possible amount or degree - the aim is to minimize cost

"But, cheating is cheating, right?"

The rational person says that, but this intellectual is going into damage control mode now with the haphazard theory of cheating by degree.

It stands to reason if something really meant nothing, you wouldn't risk losing everything for nothing.

"That's exactly what I think, but if the cheater is willing to lose everything, than it shows how important their need for attention is, right?"

Exactly! The blame game, idiotic lies and relative truths are a whole lot of work for nothing!

Allowing yourself to buy into this theory is an assault on logic.

Notes

"I can see why he/she cheated."

The crystal ball reader!

This phrase is not used by the cheater.

"Who uses it?"

The person that comes to mind is the cheat-ee!

And you can take to the bank when the shoe is on the other foot, the cheat-ee isn't going to be as clairvoyant!

Don't take this seriously, it's actually... laughable !

Notes

"Humans are not monogamous..."

Monogamy — practice or state of being married to one person ,.— the practice or state of having a sexual relationship with only one partner

Common sense tells us the cheater can't be monogamous.

If you don't feel comfortable with drama, confusion, or a high probability of contracting a venereal disease, then you might want to stay clear of the 'humans are not monogamous' person.

Bottom line is: some people have no problem with an exclusive relationship, and you can't let others put words in your mouth.

Notes

"Something different"

Any person that uses this phrase as an excuse to cheat doesn't have the wherewithal to understand a marriage contract - period.

Is it really something different or is it really ***another*** avenue of attention for them?

"Why say something this stupid?"

Cheaters throw stuff out there and hope it sticks, so obviously looking and sounding dumb really isn't a big concern for them.

Notes

"I was cheated - on"

If it's a positive frame of mind you're seeking then don't ever utter this group of words - **ever** - in regard to yourself.

"Why not use this phrase "cheated-on", that's what happened isn't it?"

No, that's not what happened.

The cheating-mate doesn't cheat **on** you, they cheat because that's what cheaters do, cheat.

"So, it's not personal?"

No it's not personal. Cheating is NOT a reflection of you - it's a reflection of the cheater!

The phrase I was cheated-on is a particularly risky one to own because it contains multiple negative implications.

You're stupid and someone got over on you.

You're unworthy of loyalty.

Something must be wrong with YOU!

"Uhhhgg I don't like that!"

Of course you don't like it and that's exactly why you need to get these words out of your mind, your mouth and your life — **forever**!

Your healing process will never work with thoughts that continuously undermine you.

Notes

"An affair is good for a marriage."

This convoluted idea was thought up by a person with a mental disorder that's often characterized by the failure to recognize what is real. Common symptoms include false beliefs, unclear or confused thinking.

"Water is good for suede" is an indisputable equivalence of "an affair is good for a marriage".

Unless a couple is in **full** agreement that each or one partner may have sexual relations with others, an affair is out-and-out injurious for the partner who would never agree to this.

Notes

"Everyone cheats."

All the other kids are doing it!!

The cheater is cavalier about this up until someone swindles them out of money.

There is only one way to view this;

Cheaters will agree that everyone cheats.

People with integrity will disagree.

This phrase is cynical.

Notes

Ok, now you have a feel for phrases that work on behalf of the cheating-mate.

Keep track - in your note pages - of negative phrases you're most vulnerable to, so you can replace them with thoughts that set you on a positive path.

There are established reactions to cheating and they are all agents of negativity.

Teaming up with these pessimistic representatives is not in your best interest!

Reinventing yourself.

Reinvent – To re-make or make over, as in a different form

"I'm going to reinvent myself so my mate will be loyal to me!"

That statement contains two misconceptions:

1. Your reinvention is based on 'getting rid' of the person you believe wasn't worthy of loyalty, and oh by the way, that's you!

2. Getting the cheaters loyalty is an oxymoron.

Personal growth is healthy, but it has to be done for the right reasons.

"What are the right reasons in this situation?"

If **you** feel you need self-improvement in some area, by all means make an outline and implement the changes,but for **you** and without an ulterior motive!

Before you make up your mind to renovate yourself, ask this question;

If my reinvention does not stop my mate from cheating will I continue it anyway?

"That question is one to really think about before I go off and change something about myself I really like just for the sake of change."

And that can happen, so think about it before you react or you may come home from the salon with spiked, peacock blue hair and an earring in your tongue!

Keep in mind that confidence is an attribute. Confidence makes us shine.

"My confidence just took a big hit; how do I boost it back without going through the rehab?"

First and foremost a loss of confidence is an old-fashioned reaction to this situation.

A silly parallel:

A bank was robbed and the police are blaming the bank for the robbery not the thieves!

You cannot allow your worth to be defined by the actions of a liar and a sneak — no reinvention will cure that!

Mantra for confidence:

I am confident: being me is enough, and I choose to be the best me that I can be. I am worthy of being respected and acknowledged, and what other people say or do won't affect the way that I view myself.

NOW ALL YOU HAVE TO DO IS BELIEVE IT!

Notes

"I want revenge!"

"He who plots to hurt others often hurts himself"

Aesop (c.620-560 BC)

When you're angry, it may seem like a good idea to whack the cheating-mate for putting you in this situation.

"Oh yes it does, and I think they should pay for what they do wrong, don't you?"

Revenge always seems like a good idea when you're angry, but inflicting pain on an individual is time consuming and it robs **you** of energy and joy.
The bad thing about revenge is it keeps you focused on someone other than yourself and that distraction interferes with your happiness building.

Remember:

Living well is the best revenge-

Calvin Tomkins

Notes

"I AM ANGRY!"

"I'm so pissed-off, I mean really pissed, I can't believe this happened to me!"

Really?

Well, you were just yanked into a situation that you don't want and haven't caused, so anger is a no brainer here!

It can be disheartening to find out that you and your mate made a commitment to each other - and you were the only one that kept it.

However, anger cannot be ignored, nor can you allow it to take over and cause you to do something you will regret.

"Ok, so what the hell can I do?"

Anger will become a terrorist in your head if you allow it to gain momentum, so you may want to consider putting a time clock on this spoiled child.

"A time clock?"

The idea behind the time clock is to nip anger in the bud before it dominates your life - you are training your emotions and thoughts.

You have to squeeze negativity out because if you don't, positive energy cannot get in!

"How much time should I start with?

The real question here is: how much time do you want to spend being pissed-off?

"None!"

Great! This is a test of your will and you must be persistent!

"Yes I must get persistent or I'll end up bitter."

You don't want that!

NOTHING can rob you of your happiness but you - your smile and joy is yours and let it shine!

Notes

Jealousy

Jealousy makes its debut primarily because you thought you were special to your mate, his/her one and only, and now you feel you're in a competition.

"Exactly, now what!"

Well, face the facts squarely and it will set you free. It's not a person the cheating-mate cheats **for** - it's their need for attention that drives them to cheat.

The cheating-mate's inadequacy is not you're competition!

"So, this could happen again and with someone else!"

It doesn't matter if it happens again and with someone else. This challenge is about your life and you are the captain of this ship!

Jealousy will weaken you and become baggage that you definitely don't want engrained in your future.

"I feel jealousy is almost unavoidable if I stay in this relationship."

Probe this question for a moment;

Will I have conquered jealousy if I leave this relationship?

"Why that question?"

The reason why this question is so important is because if you're jealous over your mate cheating that means you've let someone else's fragilities impact your self-esteem.

Breaking up a relationship over jealousy is a mistake.

"Why?"

Leaving a relationship because you're jealous won't make the jealousy go away. However, if you leave a relationship because you recognize you have a different set of values that are incompatible with your mate, you've made a rational decision - in essence you know who you are and what you want.

It's crucial to be brutally honest with yourself; it's your life, your future and your happiness.

Notes

"I am a victim!"

The 'victim mentality' will put you right in a head-prison.

"Why would you want to imprison yourself?"

The victim role works by using sympathy - manipulation. It's a guilt trip.

"Shouldn't the cheater feel guilty?"

Some may and some may not. But what's more important is the affect the victim role will have on **you**.

The main problem with this method is: it's not a hit-and-run process - it takes constant reminders and drama to keep your mate in the guilt mode, so the victim role keeps **you** locked into the pity-party as well.

No one made the cheater cheat; it was a choice, so no one can make a cheater feel guilty either way. That is also the cheater's choice.

Pity party - an instance of indulging in self-pity or eliciting pity from other people.

All in all, the victim role is a big loser because it weakens your good energy, clear thinking, and most of all your self-esteem. The victim is a person that dwells in the illusion of having 'no control' over events in their life, which isn't true, humans **always** have choices.

Do you want to be seen as confident, fun, and secure?

Or, do you want to be seen as a crybaby?
It's your choice!

Notes

Payback cheating.

"Hey, two can play this game!"

Ingenious right!

This could backfire on you.

"Really?"

First and foremost if you decide to take this route you will be giving your mate a free pass to cheat! These three words will come back to haunt you;

"Well, you do it too!"

"Yeah but he/she did it first!"

It won't matter.

Before you take the payback road, stop and ask yourself this question;

Do I want an open-marriage?

"Oh no!"

Well, the two can play this game may lead to that, so think about it.

"Hmmmmm."

This method of dealing with the cheating-mate is an act of desperation. There are predators out there that feed on this desperation and you may get taken advantage of easily because you're not thinking clearly.

"Payback cheating is not looking so good anymore."

Well, that's because you're seeing ramifications that can result from this action.

"So, I have to either fix my relationship or move on, right?"

No one can make that decision for you; however, if you decide to 'fix' your relationship, it can't be an act of force - your mate has to agree to it as well.

Before you make a serious decision, it's prudent to be aware. Negativity can be a driving force that will blur your best interests in the decision-making process.

"So, I guess the payback cheating is a knee-jerk reaction."

Payback cheating is basically becoming the very same person you're angry with.

"Don't really want to go there."

Using negative methods to repair your life is a contradiction!

Notes

Be kind to yourself

In today's world, instant gratification, degradation, confusion, and immortality have become more and more prominent in society. And, you may have even been ridiculed for your beliefs. Many people caved and sold out their integrity and courage, but also lived to regret it. Without integrity and courage we're nothing more than someone else's definition of ourselves, a programmed minion.

The relationship you have with yourself is the only relationship that matters because all your other relationships are based on that.

Right now you have found yourself in an ugly mess of uncertainty and you need to deal with it one way or the other.

Because jealousy, anger, anxiety, and confusion all have one thing in common - they are toxic poisons to your mind and body. You need to be kind to you.

"I can't eat or sleep."

Not eating or sleeping is a red flag - a warning that you have allowed negativity to control your thoughts.

No one can think straight if they don't sleep. As a matter of fact, sleep deprivation is used to extract information from terrorists; that's how dangerous it can be to the system. You're being worn down.

"Yes, I go from excited and anxious to exhaustion."

You have to calm your thoughts - period.

"I know that, I really do, but I can't seem to control it."

When faced with uncertainty, as simplistic as it may sound, it is the time to treat yourself kindly.

You can't avoid the stress that comes with uncertainty; however, you can control the ways to counter it by eating healthy meals, getting a good night's rest, and understanding that you will be ok, no matter what! Keep a positive attitude.

You're experiencing anxiety and must treat your body the same as you would if you had a cold, the flu, or an injury. Negative thoughts are toxic and they will make you ill.

"I am starting to do that right now, I didn't do anything wrong and I am not going to get sick over it!"

Now that's the right attitude!

Good luck and always keep in mind - your joy is yours and no one can rob that from you!

Smile & laugh!

Notes

www.ingramcontent.com/pod-product-compliance
Lightning Source LLC
Chambersburg PA
CBHW081522040426
42447CB00013B/3305